Date: 3/20/18

J 796.32364 BRA
Braun, Eric,
Pro basketball's underdogs :
players and teams who

PRO BASKETBALL'S

UNDERDOGS:

PLAYERS AND TEAMS WHO SHOCKED THE BASKETBALL WORLD

BY ERIC BRAUN

CAPSTONE PRESS
a capstone imprint

Sports Illustrated Kids Sports Shockers! are published by Capstone Press,
1710 Roe Crest Drive, North Mankato, Minnesota 56003
www.mycapstone.com

Library of Congress Cataloging-in-Publication data
Names: Braun, Eric, 1971- author.
Title: Pro Basketball's Underdogs : Players and Teams Who Shocked the Basketball
World / by Eric Braun.
Description: North Mankato, Minnesota. : Capstone Press, 2017. | Series: Sports
Illustrated Kids. Sports Shockers! | Includes index.
Identifiers: LCCN 2017004667| ISBN 9781515780465 (library binding) | ISBN
9781515780502 (eBook PDF)
Subjects: LCSH: Basketball--United States--History--Juvenile literature. | Basketball
players--United States--Biography--Juvenile literature.
Classification: LCC GV885.1 .B734 2017 | DDC 796.323/64--dc23
LC record available at https://lccn.loc.gov/2017004667

Editorial Credits
Nick Healy, editor; Kyle Grenz, designer; Eric Gohl, media researcher;
Kathy McColley, production specialist

Photo Credits
AP Photo: Eric Risberg, 6; Getty Images: Focus on Sport, 17, Sports Illustrated/Hank
Delespinasse, 11, Sports Illustrated/James Drake, 10, Sports Illustrated/John W.
McDonough, 14, Sports Illustrated/Manny Millan, 16; iStockphoto: OSTILL, cover
(left); Newscom: EPA/John G. Mabanglo, 7, EPA/Larry W. Smith, 4, USA Today
Sports/Troy Taormina, 8, ZUMA Press/Pool/Ronald Martinez, 5; Shutterstock: ostill,
cover (right); Sports Illustrated: Bob Rosato, 21, 25 (bottom), 31 (bottom), Damian
Strohmeyer, 18, 19, John Biever, 20, 22, 23, 28, John W. McDonough, 15, 24, 25 (top), 29,
30 (all), Manny Millan, 9, 12, 13, 26, 27, 31 (top)

Printed and bound in the USA.
010364F17

Table of Contents

Unlikely UNDERDOGS

"**C**an you imagine if we pull this off?" That question fuels every underdog story. Athletes and fans love to dream of the little guy toppling the big guy. What's more fun than that?

Consider the Cleveland Cavaliers. In the team's 45 years in the National Basketball Association (NBA), the Cavs had never won a championship. They'd come close a couple times, including in 2015, when they lost in the Finals to the sharpshooting Golden State Warriors. In Cleveland, pro sports teams had been disappointing fans for decades. No Cleveland team had hoisted a championship trophy in 52 years.

When the Cavs returned to the Finals in 2016 for a rematch with Golden State, many people expected to see Cleveland lose again. After all, the Warriors had just set a record for most regular-season wins by going 73–9. They were led by Stephen Curry, a scoring machine who had twice been named the league's most valuable player (MVP). Besides, this was Cleveland. Of course they'd lose.

The Warriors won the first two games convincingly and were up 3–1 after four games. The Cavs needed to win three in a row against a team that hadn't lost three in a row since 2013.

IN OTHER WORDS, THINGS DIDN'T LOOK GOOD.

Then the Cavs won Game 5 on the road. And they won Game 6 at home. Heading to Oakland, California, for the decisive Game 7, Cavs star LeBron James asked a friend the question: "Can you imagine if we pull this off?"

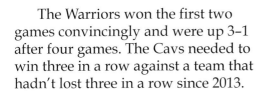

The only thing more fun than imagining an underdog's triumph is seeing it really happen.

THE CAVS WOULD SOON BECOME AN UNDERDOG STORY FOR THE AGES.

Welcome to
BELIEVELAND

The Cavaliers made their way west for Game 7 against the Golden State Warriors. A lot was riding on the muscled shoulders of LeBron James and the other players. There was more at stake than just one game. The weight of the game went beyond even the 2016 NBA Championship. The city of Cleveland itself seemed cursed.

Long-suffering Cleveland had watched its three pro sports teams come up short many times. The Cavs hadn't won a title since they came into the NBA in 1970. In baseball, the Indians hadn't won the World Series since 1948. The Browns of the National Football League hadn't won a championship since 1964.

Between the three teams, that adds up to 146 seasons without a championship. That's a heavy burden to carry, but the Cavaliers came onto the Warriors' court feeling loose and relaxed. Things would be different this time.

LeBron James scored 27 points, made 11 assists, and nabbed 11 rebounds. He also made a crucial late block, swatting away what should have been an easy Warriors layup. That block kept the score tied and set the stage for the big win.

James had been to the Finals in each of the previous five years, four with the Miami Heat. But Cleveland was his hometown. After winning the 2016 title with the Cavs—and being named the series MVP—James cried. His shoulders had helped lift the curse off of an entire city.

AN ESTIMATED 1.3 MILLION PEOPLE ATTENDED THE CAVS' VICTORY PARADE.

FACT: AFTER THE CHICAGO CUBS WON THE WORLD SERIES IN 2016, THE CLEVELAND INDIANS WERE STUCK WITH THE LONGEST TITLE DROUGHT IN PRO SPORTS. THEY HAVEN'T WON A CHAMPIONSHIP IN 68 YEARS. IN THE NBA, THE LONGEST-SUFFERING FRANCHISE IS THE SACRAMENTO KINGS, WHICH HASN'T WON A CHAMPIONSHIP SINCE 1951. BACK THEN THE TEAM WAS KNOWN AS THE ROCHESTER ROYALS.

Rise of the LITTLE GUYS

In many ways, the NBA is a big man's league. Stars like the 6-foot-10 Anthony Davis and 7-footer Karl-Anthony Towns sky for rebounds, slam down dunks, and score from all over the floor. They make "normal" guys look puny. If you are average height, it doesn't matter how sharp your skills are. You probably won't cut it in the NBA.

For a little guy, though, the word "average" looms large. Just ask Isaiah Thomas. The 5-foot-9 point guard was chosen in 2011 by the Sacramento Kings with the last pick of the draft. Thomas began his career by carving out a few decent years. But in 2014 he found himself as the third-string point guard for the Phoenix Suns. Maybe the little man had gone as far as he could.

ISAIAH THOMAS

IN FEBRUARY 2015 HE WAS TRADED TO THE BOSTON CELTICS, AND EVERYTHING CHANGED.

He quickly established himself as a star sixth man and made his first All-Star team. He led the Celtics to consecutive playoff appearances and has become the new face of the storied franchise.

Thomas knows how special his story is.

"I was the third-string point guard," he says, referring to his time with Phoenix. "Years before that, I was the sixtieth pick. A lot has changed, and it's been nice."

Thomas is special, but he's not alone. Muggsy Bogues was even shorter than Thomas. At only 5 feet 3 inches, Bogues hustled through a 14-year career, including 10 years with the Charlotte Hornets. Active from 1987 to 2001, he became the Charlotte franchise leader in multiple stat categories, including minutes played with 19,768.

MUGGSY BOGUES

FACT: ANOTHER UNDERSIZED NBA STAR WAS SPUD WEBB OF THE ATLANTA HAWKS. HE WAS ONLY 5 FEET 7 INCHES BUT HAD LEGS LIKE BOOSTER ROCKETS. WEBB WON THE 1986 SLAM DUNK CONTEST AGAINST HIS TEAMMATE, THE 6-FOOT-8 DOMINIQUE WILKINS. KNOWN AS THE "HUMAN HIGHLIGHT REEL," WILKINS HAD WON THE CONTEST THE PREVIOUS YEAR.

Shocking the SIXERS

LIONEL HOLLINS IN ACTION IN GAME 2

t's safe to say not too many people saw the 1977 World Champion Portland Trail Blazers coming. In their first six years of existence, the Blazers had never gone to the playoffs. In fact, they'd never had a winning record.

Before the 1976–77 season began, the Blazers fired their head coach and dumped seven players.

THE NEW TEAM HAD A WHOLE NEW FEEL.

The new feeling stemmed from a change of philosophy. They became selfless. They had a big star in Bill Walton, but their game didn't revolve around stars. It revolved around ball movement — sharp passing and unselfish play. "It felt like we had nothing to do with what had come before," Walton said later.

The Blazers finished the season 49–33 with a ticket to the playoffs for the first time. But nobody gave them a chance. "We were nobodies," Walton said.

Portland's fans believed, though. They filled the arena with electricity, and the players fed off that energy.

The Blazers made it to the Finals but found themselves down 2–0 to the 76ers. Philadelphia had a star-studded team led by Julius Erving — the famous Dr. J. Blazers coach Jack Ramsay held a team meeting. His message:

DON'T CHANGE A THING. WE GOT THIS.

They did. The Blazers won the next four games and made it look easy, with their passes zipping around the floor. The Philadelphia players looked confused. The team that everyone doubted had won it all.

"It was the best feeling I ever had in my life," Walton said.

FACT:
WALTON DOMINATED GAME 6, SCORING 20 POINTS, GETTING SEVEN ASSISTS, COLLECTING 23 REBOUNDS, AND SWATTING EIGHT BLOCKED SHOTS. HE WAS NAMED SERIES MVP.

BIG MAN BILL WALTON POWERS TO THE HOOP IN THE 1977 FINALS.

RODMAN REBOUNDS

As a young kid in school, Dennis Rodman was thin, shy, and weak. He was often beaten up by bigger, more aggressive kids. In high school, he got kicked off the football team and didn't make the varsity basketball team. When he graduated, he got a job as a janitor.

Rodman hadn't seen his father since he was 3 years old. He had a strained relationship with his mother. When he was arrested for stealing watches, she kicked him out of the house. Only then did Rodman consider giving basketball a serious try.

By this time he'd grown to 6 feet 7 inches, and coaches at a junior college invited him to play. It was the chance he needed. His dogged style of play made him a dominant, standout player. The Detroit Pistons drafted him in the second round in 1986.

WITH DETROIT RODMAN PLAYED IN EVERY GAME FOR FIVE SEASONS STRAIGHT.

His ferocious defense and relentless rebounding quickly turned Rodman into a star. With Rodman on board, Detroit won championships in 1989 and 1990. Rodman led the league in rebounds seven years in a row and is considered one of the greatest rebounders of all time — up there with Bill Russell and Wilt Chamberlain, both of whom were towering centers.

Rodman later played with the San Antonio Spurs and Chicago Bulls. With the Bulls, he joined Michael Jordan, winning three titles in a row.

RODMAN BECAME A STAR WITH THE PISTONS AND LATER PLAYED FOR FOUR OTHER TEAMS, FINISHING WITH SHORT STINTS WITH THE L.A. LAKERS AND DALLAS MAVERICKS.

FACT:
RODMAN FINISHED HIS CAREER WITH FIVE NBA CHAMPIONSHIPS, TWO ALL-STAR APPEARANCES, AND TWO TOP DEFENSIVE PLAYER AWARDS. HE WAS INDUCTED INTO THE NBA HALL OF FAME IN 2011.

8 BEATS 1

For a number-eight seed, the road to a championship is long and steep. Just making it out of the first playoff round is a major victory. After all, the two number-eight seeds (one from each conference) are the definition of average. They're the 15th and 16th best teams in a 30-team league. And they have to start the playoffs against one of the two top teams.

Most of the time, that works out about like you'd expect. Eighth-seeded teams tend to get slammed like an Andre Iguodala dunk. But sometimes something magical happens.

In 1994 the eighth-seeded Denver Nuggets faced the top-seeded Seattle SuperSonics, who had the league's best record that year. Denver, on the other hand, was barely over .500 at 42–40. When Seattle jumped out to a 2–0 series lead, Denver coach Dan Issel told his team they had nothing to lose and urged them to play loose and have fun.

MUTOMBO IN ACTION
AGAINST THE SONICS'
SAM PERKINS

They sure did that. The Nuggets won out, with big man Dikembe Mutombo dominating on defense.

IT WAS THE FIRST TIME AN EIGHT HAD BEATEN A ONE IN NBA HISTORY.

The Nuggets lost to the Utah Jazz in the next round. Still, their underdog win had broken new ground.

In 1999 the New York Knicks became the first eight-seed to make the Finals, where they fell to the San Antonio Spurs.

In 2007 the Golden State Warriors knocked off the one-seed Dallas Mavericks in seven games, only to lose to the Utah Jazz in the next round.

Today top seeds do not take a first-round win for granted.

WARRIORS GUARD BARON DAVIS AVERAGED MORE THAN 25 POINTS PER GAME IN THE 2007 PLAYOFFS.

FACT:
THE KNICKS WOULD BE SEEDED THIRD IN 2000 AND GO TO THE FINALS AGAIN, ONLY TO LOSE ONCE MORE, THIS TIME TO THE INDIANA PACERS.

The Washington OPERA

The Washington Bullets had gone to the NBA Finals twice during the 1970s, and they had lost both times. There was little reason for hope during the 1977–78 season, which the Bullets finished with a just-okay record of 44–38. Heading into the postseason, they were self-proclaimed underdogs. To win it all, they would have to defeat some high-powered teams, while never having home-court advantage.

NEW COACH DICK MOTTA FORGED A NEVER-SAY-DIE ATTITUDE WITH THE TEAM. "THE OPERA AIN'T OVER 'TILL THE FAT LADY SINGS," HE SAID.

Washington (now the Wizards) defeated the favored Spurs in the second round and knocked off the even-more-favored 76ers in the third round. In the Finals, they faced the Seattle SuperSonics.

The Sonics swiped Game 1, roaring back after trailing by 19 points. The Washington media didn't seem to believe in its team and kept reminding them of their previous failures in the Finals. When they did, Motta reminded them to wait for the fat lady.

Throughout the series, Bullets center Wes Unseld played a highly physical game. His numbers weren't eye-popping, but the Sonics could not handle his bone-shattering picks and crushing defense.

"THAT'S OUR GAME," MOTTA SAID.

The series went down to the wire. In Game 7, Unseld made two free throws with 12 seconds left in the fourth quarter to seal the Bullets' 105–99 win. Washington finally had its first title.

BIG MEN WES UNSELD (41) AND JACK SIKMA BATTLED IN THE PAINT.

LINSANITY!

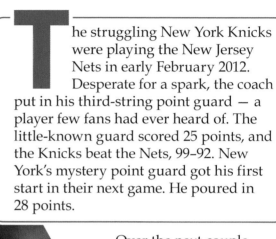

The struggling New York Knicks were playing the New Jersey Nets in early February 2012. Desperate for a spark, the coach put in his third-string point guard — a player few fans had ever heard of. The little-known guard scored 25 points, and the Knicks beat the Nets, 99–92. New York's mystery point guard got his first start in their next game. He poured in 28 points.

Over the next couple weeks, he started 12 games and averaged 22.5 points. And the Knicks, who had been 8–15 before this run, went 9–3. Hardly anyone knew who this player was before, but now everybody — everybody — was talking about him.

WHO WAS THIS GUY?

He was Jeremy Lin. He'd gone to Harvard, a university known for its academics much more than its sports. After going undrafted, Lin had signed as a free agent with Golden State. He played sparingly his first two years, was cut twice, and was eventually claimed by New York to cover for injuries.

Then Lin went on a tear so unbelievable that people labeled it "Linsanity."

How did a player this good avoid notice for so long? Why hadn't he gotten a chance before? At least part of the reason is that he is an Asian-American playing a sport that relatively few Asian-Americans play.

"The fact that I'm Asian-American makes it harder to believe, even crazier, more unexpected," Lin said.

Lin got a big contract from the Houston Rockets the following year and has played for the L.A. Lakers, the Charlotte Hornets, and the Brooklyn Nets. His numbers didn't stay at Linsanity levels, but he has been a dynamic and successful player for years. Not bad for an underdog from the end of the bench.

MORE OUT-OF-NOWHERE SPORTS STARS:

KURT WARNER WAS STOCKING GROCERIES ONLY MONTHS BEFORE BECOMING A DOMINANT NFL QUARTERBACK AND WINNING THE SUPER BOWL.

FERNANDO VALENZUELA WAS A PITCHER FROM A TINY TOWN IN MEXICO. AT AGE 20 IN 1981, HE STARTED OUT 8-0 FOR THE LOS ANGELES DODGERS, WON THE CY YOUNG AS A ROOKIE, AND SPARKED "FERNANDOMANIA."

BILLY RAY BATES SIGNED A 10-DAY CONTRACT WITH THE PORTLAND TRAIL BLAZERS IN 1980 AND IMMEDIATELY BECAME A SCORING MACHINE. HE HELPED THE BLAZERS SQUEAK INTO THE PLAYOFFS.

Powered by TEAMWORK

When the Detroit Pistons traded for center Ben Wallace in 2000, it was seen mostly as a way to save money. The team had not gotten past the first round of the playoffs in nine years and had missed them altogether in four of the past eight. It was time to slash payroll and rebuild with cheaper players.

It worked. Wallace developed into a force on defense. A couple years later, Detroit hired coach Larry Brown and signed center Rasheed Wallace. The pieces were finally in place for the underdog Pistons to go deep into the playoffs.

The Pistons finished the 2003–04 season at 54–28 and made it to the Eastern Conference Finals. They faced the Indiana Pacers, a team that could not adjust to Detroit's controlled-tempo game. Detroit won the series and went to the Finals for the first time since 1990. Their opponents were the heavily favored Los Angeles Lakers, who had won three of the last four NBA championships.

CHAUNCEY BILLUPS DRIVES TO THE HOOP IN THE 2004 FINALS

L.A. featured a cast of superstars, including Shaquille O'Neal, Kobe Bryant, Karl Malone, and Gary Payton. But compared to the Pistons' team-first philosophy, the Lakers played like a group of selfish stars. Detroit's team-oriented defense smothered the Lakers throughout the series, and L.A. couldn't handle their pass-first offense. Detroit won the series in a walk, four games to one.

BILLUPS PLAYED FOR FOUR TEAMS IN HIS FIRST FIVE PRO SEASONS BEFORE LEADING THE PISTONS TO A CHAMPIONSHIP.

"THEY MAY HAVE HAD BETTER INDIVIDUAL PLAYERS, BUT WE ALWAYS FELT WE WERE A BETTER TEAM,"

Pistons guard Chauncey Billups said after Detroit closed it out.

FACT:

THE PISTONS WERE NO LONGER UNDERDOGS THE FOLLOWING YEAR, AND THEY MARCHED THEIR WAY TO THE 2005 FINALS. THEY LOST A HARD-FOUGHT SERIES TO THE SAN ANTONIO SPURS. THE PISTONS FINISHED THE FOLLOWING SEASON WITH A FRANCHISE BEST 64-18 RECORD BUT FAILED TO MAKE IT TO THE FINALS.

HAIRY
Story

The 10th of 11 siblings, Ben Wallace didn't have a lot of spending money as a young kid. But he learned to cut hair, and soon he was charging $3 a cut. With his savings, he went to a basketball camp run by New York Knicks star Charles Oakley.

Wallace wanted to be a slick passer like Magic Johnson and an offensive force like Michael Jordan. Oakley taught him to use his big body to play a more physical game instead.

Wallace turned down a football scholarship to play hoops at a community college, then transferred to Virginia Union University. There, Wallace began to hone his game.

HE TURNED HIMSELF INTO A REBOUNDING, SHOT-BLOCKING BRUISER.

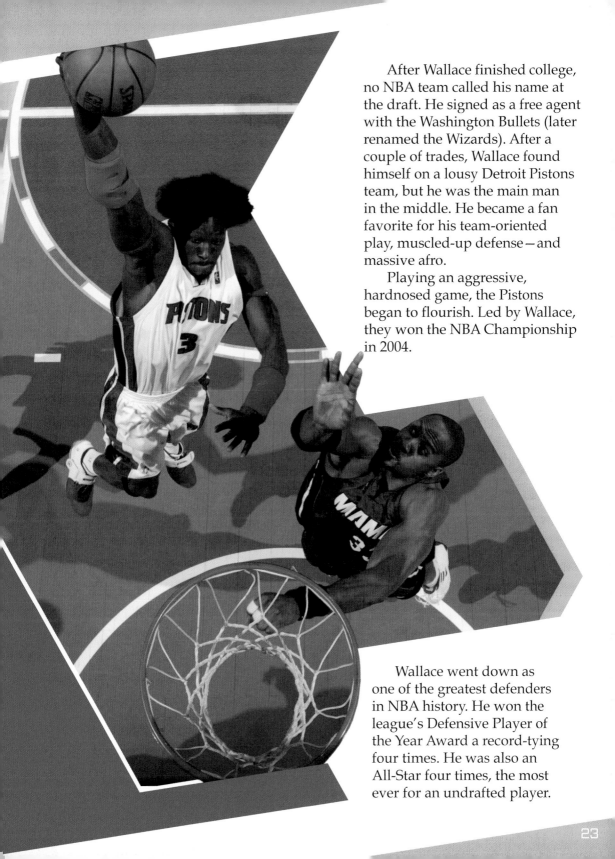

After Wallace finished college, no NBA team called his name at the draft. He signed as a free agent with the Washington Bullets (later renamed the Wizards). After a couple of trades, Wallace found himself on a lousy Detroit Pistons team, but he was the main man in the middle. He became a fan favorite for his team-oriented play, muscled-up defense—and massive afro.

Playing an aggressive, hardnosed game, the Pistons began to flourish. Led by Wallace, they won the NBA Championship in 2004.

Wallace went down as one of the greatest defenders in NBA history. He won the league's Defensive Player of the Year Award a record-tying four times. He was also an All-Star four times, the most ever for an undrafted player.

Steal of the DRAFT

As a kid, Manu Ginóbili loved watching the NBA, and he loved to play basketball. But Manu and his family lived in Argentina. Only two Argentine players had ever played in the NBA. On top of that, Manu was smaller than his peers and not considered an elite talent. He was a long way from the NBA.

But Ginóbili began to sprout up in his late teens. At the age of 18, he made his pro debut in Argentina during the 1995–96 season. Two years later he led the Argentinian League in scoring. He moved to the EuroLeague, where he played with an Italian team for two years.

He was still a long way from the NBA, but the San Antonio Spurs had their eye on him. In the 1999 draft, they chose him with the 57th overall selection.

Ginóbili did not sign with the Spurs that year. He returned to Italy to play for Kinder Bologna. The team won the 2001 Italian League Championship, the 2001 and 2002 Italian Cups, and the 2001 EuroLeague. Ginóbili was named the MVP of the EuroLeague and the EuroLeague Finals.

GINÓBILI GOES TO THE HOOP.

Ginóbili finally signed with the Spurs for the 2002–03 season. When the season began, he was nursing an injured ankle and didn't play much. Ginóbili got healthy toward the end of the year and was named Rookie of the Month for March. San Antonio went 14–3 that month, while Ginóbili averaged 10.6 points, 3.3 assists, 3.1 rebounds, and 2.24 steals.

In the playoffs Ginóbili was on the floor regularly. The Spurs romped to a championship, beating the New Jersey Nets in the Finals. Ginóbili was an unforeseen threat to opponents, especially on defense, where he racked up 41 steals in the postseason.

Ginóbili went on to be a star in the United States and at home in Argentina, playing a crucial role in four Spurs' championships. As a two-time All-Star who was chosen 57th (of 58 picks) in the draft, he is considered perhaps the greatest "Steal of the Draft" in NBA history.

FACT:

GINÓBILI IS ONE OF TWO PLAYERS TO HAVE WON A EUROLEAGUE TITLE, AN NBA CHAMPIONSHIP, AND AN OLYMPIC GOLD MEDAL. HE STARRED FOR ARGENTINA'S GOLD-MEDAL TEAM IN THE 2004 GAMES IN ATHENS, GREECE.

Rockets POWER

The Hakeem Olajuwon-led Rockets of 1993–94 won the Finals with a simple formula: feed the big guy in the paint and defend like crazy. They played consistent ball, and they won it all. So how come the 1994–95 Rockets, who returned with almost the same team, were underdogs?

Injuries and suspensions of key players hurt them. And the burden of high expectations seemed to weigh them down. They started strong but began to stumble — badly — and needed to make a change. In January they did. The team traded for Clyde Drexler. Clyde the Glide, as he was known, joined Olajuwon, and the two quickly jelled into a super-duo. That was no great surprise. They had been teammates in college, after all.

OLAJUWON RANKS AS ONE OF THE TOP CENTERS IN NBA HISTORY.

The Rockets made up a lot of ground and finished the regular season 47–35. They headed into the 1995 playoffs as the sixth seed in the Western Conference. The Rockets faced a tough climb. They would not have home-court advantage in the postseason.

NO SIXTH SEED HAD EVER WON THE CHAMPIONSHIP.

But Houston pulled it off. On the way, they defeated four teams — the Utah Jazz, Phoenix Suns, Orlando Magic, and San Antonio Spurs — that had all won at least 57 games. Dating back to the previous season, the Rockets ran up an unprecedented string of winning eight straight elimination games. It was the most difficult path to an NBA championship any team had ever traveled.

DREXLER WAS A SUPERSTAR IN PORTLAND BEFORE BEING DEALT TO THE ROCKETS.

FACT:

BEFORE GAME 2 OF THE FINALS IN SAN ANTONIO, THE LEAGUE GAVE DAVID ROBINSON OF THE SPURS HIS LEAGUE MVP AWARD. ROBINSON HOISTED THE TROPHY MERE FEET FROM THE ROCKETS BENCH. DREXLER, WHO BELIEVED OLAJUWON DESERVED THE AWARD, WAS STEAMED AT THE DISRESPECT. BUT OLAJUWON TOLD HIM NOT TO WORRY. "WE WILL GET THE BIG TROPHY," OLAJUWON TOLD HIS TEAMMATE. "I FELT REALLY GOOD AT THAT POINT," DREXLER LATER RECALLED.

MAKING a SPLASH

With a dad who was an NBA veteran, maybe Stephen Curry doesn't sound like an underdog. That seems obvious after fans have seen him win two MVP Awards, go to consecutive NBA Finals, and set records for three-pointers.

But at 6 feet and 160 pounds, Curry was considered too small to play Division I basketball, much less in the pros. After high school, the scrawny sharpshooter wasn't offered a scholarship to any of the big basketball schools. Instead, he settled for Davidson College, a little-known school in North Carolina. There, he built on his already solid reputation as a great shooter, but he continued to face doubts. Could a wiry guy like Curry — by now he stood 6-foot-3 but was still thin — make it in the physical world of the NBA?

CURRY LED DAVIDSON TO THE ELITE 8 IN 2008, KNOCKING OFF POWERFUL PROGRAMS ALONG THE WAY.

The Golden State Warriors took a chance, selecting him with the seventh pick in the 2009 draft. The first few years of his career, Curry battled injuries. He played fine when he was on the court, but he wasn't yet a superstar.

In 2014–15, finally healthy and working with new coach Steve Kerr, Curry began to emerge as a force. He and teammate Klay Thompson, also a long-bomb specialist, were nicknamed the "Splash Brothers." Why? Because the sight of their shots splashing the net was so common. That year Curry set the record for most three-point shots in a season. He also won the league MVP and led his team to its first championship since 1975.

FACT:
CURRY'S FATHER, DELL CURRY, WAS ALSO A THREE-POINT SPECIALIST. HE HOLDS THE CHARLOTTE HORNETS FRANCHISE RECORD FOR MOST THREES AS WELL AS MOST POINTS OVERALL.

Underdog ROUNDUP

Bruce Bowen: He went undrafted by the NBA and started his career playing in France. He finally caught on with the 1997 Heat. Eventually he forged a 12-year career — mostly with the Spurs — as one of the greatest defenders ever. San Antonio retired his jersey number in 2012.

2010-11

Dallas Mavericks: The Miami Heat had their newly formed "big three" of LeBron James, Dwayne Wade, and Chris Bosh. They were expected to cruise to a Finals victory and establish a new dynasty. Instead, the Mavericks duo of Dirk Nowitzki and Jason Terry led Dallas to a surprise 4–2 Finals victory.

John Starks: Starks, who grew up in extreme poverty, played only two games of varsity basketball in high school. He worked as a stocker in a grocery store and bounced to several colleges before going undrafted by any NBA team. Eventually he signed with Golden State, but the Warriors later cut him. He finally landed with the New York Knicks. He became an NBA All-Star in 1994 and was awarded the league's Sixth Man of the Year in 1996–97.

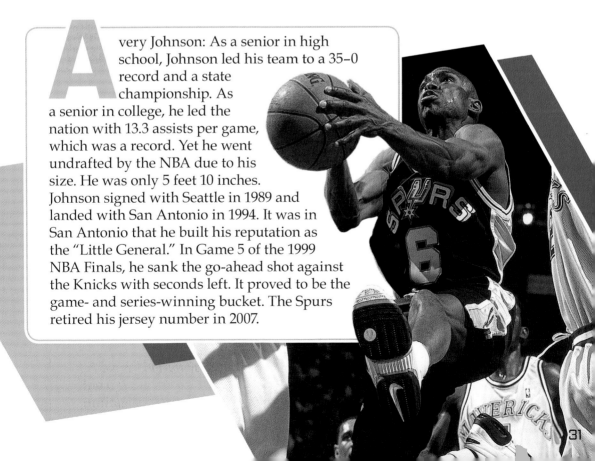

Avery Johnson: As a senior in high school, Johnson led his team to a 35–0 record and a state championship. As a senior in college, he led the nation with 13.3 assists per game, which was a record. Yet he went undrafted by the NBA due to his size. He was only 5 feet 10 inches. Johnson signed with Seattle in 1989 and landed with San Antonio in 1994. It was in San Antonio that he built his reputation as the "Little General." In Game 5 of the 1999 NBA Finals, he sank the go-ahead shot against the Knicks with seconds left. It proved to be the game- and series-winning bucket. The Spurs retired his jersey number in 2007.

READ MORE

Bryant, Howard. *Legends: The Best Players, Games, and Teams in Basketball.* New York: Philomel Books, 2016.

The Editors of Sports Illustrated Kids. *Sports Illustrated Kids Big Book of Who Basketball.* New York: Sports Illustrated, 2015.

Frederick, Shane. *Basketball's Record Breakers.* North Mankato, Minn.: Capstone Press, 2017.

INTERNET SITES

Use FactHound to find Internet sites related to this book.

Visit www.facthound.com

Just type in 9781515780465 and go.

INDEX